SAP HR Interview Questions, Answers, and Explanations

By SAPCOOKBOOK.COM

Please visit our website at www.sapcookbook.com

ISBN 0-9753052-5-5

The programs in this book have been included for instructional value only. They have been tested with care but are not guaranteed for any particular purpose. The publisher does not offer any warranties or representations not does it accept any liabilities with respect to the programs.

Trademark notices

SAP, SAP EBP, SAP SRM, Netweaver, and SAP New Dimension are registered trademarks of SAP AG. This publisher gratefully acknowledges SAP permission to use its trademark in this publication. SAP AG is not the publisher of this book and is not responsible for it under any aspect of the law.

Motivation

During the course of an average project, I am usually
called upon by a project manager to "help screen
resources" for different parts of the project. And one
thing comes to mind – if done properly, it's very time
consuming, and it's really hard work!

My interviews usually sound something like this –

Jim: "Please rate yourself, on a scale of 1-10 on your HR
knowledge and experience..."

Interviewee: "Um, probably something like 10..."

Jim: "OK, so, let me just say something... I don't believe
there is such a thing as a ten."

Interviewee: "What would you rate yourself?"

Jim: "I rate myself an 8."

Interviewee: "Why so low?"

Jim: "There's no such thing as a ten. All of the nines are
working at SAP, SAP Labs, or SAP Consulting, and so
basically that puts me at about an eight. But we're here
to talk about *your* skills. And so you think you're a 10,
huh? OK, so tell me what you know about debugging the
n-step approval workflow..."

And then I try to ask the questions that truly flesh out a
person's understanding of the software. It's part science,
part art to be sure – but the #1 thing I'm looking for in

an interview is that the resource represents their skills truthfully. The good resources know what they know, know what they don't know, and they're open about it.

And so I hope that this book will serve as a much-needed guide for managers trying to get the right resource for their project. If you construct an interview based on these questions, I'm confident you can get a good idea about the depth and breadth of a consultant's experiences and accumulated knowledge.

SAPCOOKBOOK.COM

August 2005

Introduction

This book is divided into three parts – configuration related questions, technical and troubleshooting questions, and finally, transaction code and table references, plus an index that will help you quickly find the information that you're looking for.

Each interview question has a question and an answer – that is pretty straightforward – but when you see the guru icon – this is information that represents the highest degree of knowledge in a particular area. So if you're looking for a "workflow guru" be sure to listen for an answers similar to those given under the guru icon.

 Don't be bamboozled!

The HR Guru has Spoken!

Part I: Configuration Related Questions

Question 1: Payroll Results

How do you post the payroll results to FICO? I created one symbolic account and assigned the same to Salaries GL Account and then completed the other configuration steps needed to complete the procedure. However, when I tried to run the simulation for posting to FICO, I got the message "Document is not generated".

A: If you have selected "Output Log" at the beginning of your configuration procedure, it will tell you at the bottom part what went wrong.

Question 2: Wage Components

What is the basis of valuation of certain wage components such as Provident Fund? Where does one configure it? A corollary question is what if another component – i.e., Special Allowance is made as basis of calculation at another time? How is this configured?

A: Go to view V_T511 wage type char and read the F1 help for field Indirect Evaluation module. Module PRZNT will be applicable in this case. Also read help for V_T539J. Both these nodes can be found under Payroll Date>Basic Pay.

Question 3: Deduction Wage Type

We have a deduction wage type displayed in the window of our pay slip that shows a negative value. This causes problems and we have tried several measures to correct this including conversion rule 16 for our wage type in the same window but so far, without any success. How can we correct or delete the negative sign?

A: You can review OSS Note 406977. This is a collective note of issues with RPCEDTx0 with examples of problems and solutions.

Question 4: Payroll Simulation

How do I correct the payroll simulation entry and check the correctness of our master data? What if one hundred employees get rejected due to error 167-process health plans. What does the following error mean?

"No entry for plan DENT/cost variant. FMDN/key////x00000000000000"

A: You should check for the cost element associated and the validity of cost rule for this plan. To do this, check your configuration under Benefits>Plans>Health Plans>Define cost variant and define cost rules.

Question 5: Leave Quota

How do I make sure that if an employee goes over the limit of a leave quota, the future leave accrual will be reflected accurately?

A: Configure the negative deduction and check these through the rules.

Question 6: Compensatory Time

How do I configure employees' compensatory time off within the same month? How do you configure ½ day off for 4 hours that the employee worked on during holidays or days off? How about an employee who worked for more than 7 hours that should have an equivalent one day off to be offset within the same month?

A: Configuration should be done through rules only. Write a rule that checks for day type1 including employees' presence. If yes, get the number of hours worked. If this is >4, add 0.5 to a time type. Set the value of the time type as 0 at the start of every month. When an employee comes for a compensatory time off, execute the report PT_ERL00 and check if the type has sufficient balance. If no, reject the compensatory time off. If yes, create an absence type for compensatory time off.

You can also use another rule of reducing the value of the time type with the compensation time off absence type.

Question 7: Wage Type Leave Allowance

How do I set the values or customize wage type as "Leave Allowance" that is paid to an employee as validated in Infotype 0014? How do I make sure that whenever there is a work schedule change, it won't run prorated? And last, if there is a resignation during the middle of the month, how do I make sure that the configuration prorates the changes?

A: Check with the "Factoring and Storage" subschema and check the rule that generates the monthly factors. The operations in this rule determine how each of the wage type in the /801 to /809 series is derived.

The way in which factors /801 to /809 are calculated tends to be specific to each implementation.

Question 8: HR Year End

What are the HR year end updates that need to be done for a US client (ver.4.70)? Do we need to apply all HRSPs available in the market? What preparations and precautions should be done?

A: SAP has released two Year End OSS Notes Phase 1 – 860792 in HRSP 47 and Phase II – 890833 in HRSP 49 (which is due for release on 12/13/2005). You have to apply these 2 notes as they include legal changes. For further information, please check the above OSS notes.

Question 9: Compensation Plan

How do you configure a basic compensation plan for an employee subgroup?

A: After creating and distributing the budget, execute the liberation. Verify that everything in the organizational units do exist and are linking to an object type BU.

Question 10: Upgrading HR

I am currently working in an upgrade project from 4.5B to ERP. Whenever I do testing actions or qualifications in the Development client, a transport request is set off. How do I turn this off?

A: Check table T77So (system table). Then check values for TRSP ADMIN and TRSP CORR. Most likely, they have been set to blank, meaning that automatic transport selection is activated for PD objects. Set the values to X.

Question 11: More Year End

Our Company is trying to run a year-end test for the 2005-06 tax year. We have encountered some errors before and have fixed most of them except for this one:

"T5635F Tax Reference"

What does the message means? When will the new 2006 constants be available?

A: Unfortunately, it is not possible to generate an XML for this tax year (2005). It is because HMRC made extensive changes to the business rules for 2005-06. You can refer to this website as reference:

http://www.hmrc.gov.uk/ebu/paye_techpack/eoy-2006-businessrules-v3.0.pdf

In a user group conference, HMRC state that hopefully employers will be able to submit files for testing from march 2006. In the meantime, you can produce test files for 2004-05 tax year. You could also produce ALV outputs of your EoY figures for 2005-06.

Meanwhile, the changes to e-filing will be done in note 895222. It is expected to be delivered in January HRSP. Therefore, creating an XML file will not be possible until January 2006.

Question 12: Creating new infotypes

Is there any manual or document available on how to create a new infotype in SAP HR?

A: You can go to the SAP Library, and then proceed to HR Tools. In this section, you can find a document for developing PA and PD Infotypes.

Question 13: IT0015

I need to capture a reason in additional payment IT0015. The reason code is "save" in this infotype. I tried to capture for reason A Example to ADDWT 9999 if Reason ADDWT9998. How can I check the reason in IT0015 for accuracy?

A: You can try using this to start with:

'TABLEP0015> VARGBPREAS'

Then, use the variable key to define the different reasons.

Question 14: Parameter 1

When we try to use BREAK statement in a schema, it is expecting Parameter 1 entry. What should we define in Parameter 1?

A: Parameter 1 is your ABAP prefix. You can et this by using PID 'AB4'. One example would be : System>User Profile>Own Data>Parameters.

Question 15: Wagetype Adjustment

Is there an adjustment wagetype for EOY figures for Ireland payroll that can process RT figures without impacting other payroll results?

A: There is no specific Irish standard from SAP but you can create your own.

Question 16: Leave Credits

How do you configure quota accrual of leave credits every six months?

A: If you are using IT0041, you can write PCR in the time evaluation to incorporate IT0041 and check for the year of services. Quota will then automatically accrue when time evaluation is run during the specified date of accrual. Use months instead of years for an indicator for more precise calculations.

Question 17: Change Management

We are trying to add a configuration wherein the users will be able to create the queries directly in a QA environment without creating in DEV and then transporting it to QA. How can this be accomplished even as the QA is locked from configuration changes?

A: It appears that you are using a "global area" (i.e. cross-client) infoset. This will not allow changes in a locked down system. What you can do is copy your global area infoset to a standard area infoset (i.e. client-specific), and this should work for your requirements.

Question 18: Payroll Simulation

Why is the system not picking up the values changed this month by default during payroll simulation? However, when I tried last month's retro date, it picks up correctly. How can this issue be corrected?

A: You can check the "Earliest MD change" date on infotype 0003. If you have done that already and payroll simulation still doesn't function by default, then there is a problem with your infotype and/or wage type retro settings. Check table T582A.

Question 19: Payroll Classes

I have completed the payroll configuration and the processing classes are also defined. However, when I tried running the payroll in RT tables, none of the wagetypes or entries can be seen in the process. Instead the RT table is showing all technical wagetypes with junk value. What could be the problem?

A: You can check your cumulation classes, and the value of processing classes 03, 20 and 30.

Question 20: Single Payroll

Is it possible to configure a single payroll to pay an individual in multiple currencies?

A: No. The system can be configured to pay in multiple currencies but not to pay an individual in multiple currencies.

Question 21: Time Evaluation

While running Time Evaluation, we are getting feedback:

'No entry in table T511K 40 TETOL 01'.

'Technical error no. 72.'

We are implementing +ve time management, and the country group is 40. Should we maintain entry in T511K for TETOL constant?

A: Yes. This is the tolerance time and has to be configured based on your requirement. As of now, create a constant with value 8 and proceed. It should work. In case it throws another error 'TGMAX not maintained' – this denotes the daily maximum working time and should be defined accordingly.

Question 22: Other benefits

How can I add in a wage type in IR8A appendix 8A under 'K Other benefits' which do not fall within the above items?

A: Modify the Evaluation class for that wagetype in Table V_512W_D Evaluation class-7. Input as 'D9 – Other benefits' which do not fall within the above limits.

Question 23: Deleting Employees

Is it possible to configure our training module in HR-SAP to automatically delete an employee who either separate or get terminated from our company just before a scheduled training or conference?

A: No. SAP does not provide an employees name to be automatically be deleted from a pre-booking list. A possible solution is to execute the following:

1. Revise business process and make HR administrator responsible for checking pre-bookings for the personnel leaving and to take them off the list manually.

2. A user exit which can display a message in 'Leaver action' after performing operation 'Save>change>delimit, etc.' on the last infotype in the action sequence, display an appropriate message to bring the administrators' attention to update pre-booking list. However, manual maintenance of pre-booking list should still continue.

Question 24: Employee Wages

How do I configure an employee's wages if she performs two functions in one office? She is currently due a shift differential in one position but not on the second one. Would changing the configuration of Personnel Calculation Rules (PCR) be involved? If so, how is this done?

A: Time Evaluation should create the wagetypes for the correct hours based on the time input. If this is not configured, it would involve creating new rules for shift differential. You can also consider using infotype 2003. This should allow change to both positions and daily work schedules.

Question 25: ECC 5.0

How do you configure the ECC 5.0 to generate vacancy assignment infotype based on the inheritance from an earlier ad placed on the system?

A: For 5.0 to automatically take care of the vacancy assignment infotype, do the following:

Declare position as vacant – open;

Assign vacancy to advertisement;

Assign ad to applicant during initial entry;

Vacancy evaluation reports will show you vacancy details and status.

Question 26: Locking Infotypes

Is it possible to create a locked infotype record via a BDC session?

A: You can try using authorization D and E for the infotype.

Question 27: Wagetype Processing

How can I configure a wagetype processing class with the following characteristics?

1. Does not withold federal and state tax.

2. Witholds Social Security and Medicare.

A: The simplest way is to copy existing wagetype that works like the same way. Your payroll should be able to identify one that will work for you. After identification, use transaction PU30 to copy the wagetype.

Question 28: Manual Overtime Approval

Is there a method to enable the user to approve overtime manually (or by message processing) through pmtw or inbox?

A: CATS is used to approve overtimes manually. If you want SAP to automatically consider the clock-in and clock-out for approval, then go in for 2007 infotype. This is the only infotype used to approve overtime. If the clock-in and clock-out shows 4 hours and of the supervisor has entered 3 hours in 2007 infotype, then the system will take only 3 hours (whichever is less from 2007 and 2011). You just need to create an attendance quota of type 01 and just have this function in schema TM00. Except for overtime, SAP has made other things difficult to configure in time management.

Question 29: User management

We have about 900 users and 70 Superusers. Is there a way to prevent users from deleting critical infotype records? Is there a specific approach either through standard SAPHR security or customization to prevent this?

A. You can introduce a customer-specific authorization check (AUTSW-NNNNN). Implement BAdI "Business Add-In HR: Authorization Check (HRPAD00AUTH_Check)". Then: IMG: PM→ PA→Tools→Authorization Management.

Question 30: HR Integration

I am a beginner with SAP and have reached the integration part. I need help understanding the flow configuration as to how to start the integration between OM to PA, OM to Recruitment and PA to Recruitment.

A: OM to PM requires switch PLOGI ORGA to be set to "X" in table T77So. Also set PLOGI to your plan version (usually 01) and set feature PLOGI to "X" for relevant groupings of employees.

PA to recruitment requires features PRELR, PRELI and PAPLI to be configured.

Question 31: Payroll Wage types

How can I configure the payroll so that the value of each employee wagetype can be found in one place?

A: You could start with V_T511K as this will hold payroll constants. From there, you can use the constant in a rule.

You can also avoid having to assign a cash value in each case by using valuation module CONST and configuration of table T510K. You can then quickly load against employee records using fast entry, or a CATT script.

Question 32: Best Date for Hiring

In using SAP HR, which is better – using the hire date or using the conversion date?

A: It is far easier to choose a "conversion" date rather than the original hire date. Provided that you have configured feature ENTRY to run off the relevant date type on infotype 0041 which defines the original hire date, you should not have any problems with this approach.

If you intend to load history, etc., be sure to choose a conversion date which will allow for the loading of historic data.

Question 33: Employee Subgroups

I am currently using a v4.6c. With this, is it possible to default different Employee Subgroups for different hiring actions?

A: No, it's not possible to use any configuration on actions.

My suggestion would be to make use of the user exits available in PA – zxpadu01 or 02.

Another option is to load them against the position – that way they will default from there.

Question 34: Quota Computation

How do I compute quota by using dynamic action? Is it possible to delimit period and compute a new quota? Do I need special switches or special definitions in order to accomplish this?

A: Let your requirement be driven through quota corrections. Instead of populating the absence quotas infotype, populate the quota corrections infotype and leave it to the time evaluation to populate the absence quotas infotype.

Question 35: Screen Header

Is it possible to configure the screen header on the PA30/PA40 screen the same way you would for any infotype?

A: Yes it is. Look at the IMG:

Personnel management → personnel Administration → Customizing User Interfaces → Change Screen Header.

Question 36: New Hire Action

What defaults should I use for initial recording of an initial hire action in SAP? Should I use the actual values or some default values like 9999, etc.?

A: There are two commonly used options for this:

1) Load the employees with their current assignment of EG, ESG, PA and PSA.

2) Configure new values for EG, ESG, PA and PSA and label them as "migration only" or "historic data load" (the text is up to you). Then hire all employees to these values.

Question 37: PCR Accumulation

How can I write a PCR to accumulate the hours and amount so I can pass it on to another PCR?

A: If you have the same WT passed through the payroll more than once in the same pay period, then you could either cumulate the total value in an output WT or a Variable WT.

Then, use this newly generated WT in the PCR in place of 2000.

Part II: Technical and Troubleshooting Questions

Question 38: Uploading Excel Files

How do you upload an excel file into infotype 21 for a group of employees utilizing the CATT (Computer Aided Testing Tool)?

A: You can download a step by step guide to record the CATT data upload program of HR data from Excel to SAP through various third party programs.

Question 39: Enter New Hire

How do I enter a new hire to PA40 in the Infotype 0000? I cannot seem to enter the position and no defaults appear, instead organizational units appear.

A: Take note that the checkbox for "P" should be selected for hiring Action in table T529A.

Question 40: Screen Modification

I am encountering some problems with Infotype Screen Modification. I have created a simple Infotype containing three (3) fields. One of these fields is intended to be a checkbox. To accomplish this, I have deleted the field and recreated it as a checkbox. But when I tried to process the infotype in pa30, the field I had modified is disabled. Where did I go wrong in the process?

A: There is a probability that you have not assigned the field to the correct modification group. You can retrace your steps by initially checking that the field is described as an output field. Then, check modification group 01. Make sure that the value is "006" for the checkbox to be an input field.

Question 41: P60 Form

We have been looking at the P60 and have concluded that we need to amend it to ensure that we can place the address on the stationary as it is meant to be folded in a "Z" pattern. Can we amend the form so we could have the employee address on top and to ensure that the stationary folds properly?

A: For any amendment to the SAP standard P60, you will need to have it approved by HRMC however minor. Once amendments have been approved, be aware that you need to compare the SAP standard P60 each year with your amended copy to make sure all changes are incorporated.

Question 42: Customizing PAW1

Can the transaction PAW1 be customized?

A: Yes. The transaction PAW1 is used in ESS for the service "Who is who". PZ01 is the transaction through which you can access the customization table for the PWA1. Select the country and enter. It will take you to the Screen where you can then make the changes you need.

Question 43: Fast Entry

How do you use PA70 and Infotype 2010 in PA70 fast entry screen without losing the WBS element and Order# fields that I added?

A: You can create a variant of the standard screen for fast entry and add the relevant fields to the view. Use the following procedure:

Within the IMG use Personnel management>Personnel Administration>Customizing Use Interfaces>Change Screen Modifications to create a new screen variant. Then use Personnel Management>Personnel Administration>Customizing Procedures>Infotype Menus to point PA70 to the new variant.

To avoid any unwanted items from showing up, you need to update the feature linked to the screen in T588M – Infotype Screen Control. Check out the help associated with this item in the IMG.

Question 44: Infotype PA61

Does PA61 Infotype 2052 update Infotype 2001 and 2002 only?

A: Yes. Maintaining time data using the weekly calendar is another method for fast entry of employee data. This method allows you to create several data records for an employee in any one week. You can also track the distribution of the employees' attendance hours on a weekly basis. In addition, specifications for Controlling and Materials management can be maintained in all weekly calendar screens. Weekly calendar screen provide for the following Infotypes: Absences (2001) and Attendance (2002)

You can also enter the most important specifications and assignments in the weekly calendar. These include: Cost assignment, Activity Allocation, External Services, Company Code, and others.

Question 45: Automated Tab Control

How can a user utilizing 4 tabs complete a data entry in first tab1 screen and save it without closing the Infotype screen?

A: The solution is to explore the options of tab strip control (Paging in the GUI and Paging in the application server). Use the first option and finally create a button to exit the screen and come to the main screen. At the click of the button, fire the code to take the content from the GUI and push it to the database.

Question 46: Small HR Department

How do we implement the SAP HR program in our company with only two people in the HR department? We are currently implementing processes for five areas of HR BOK (HR Body of Knowledge). The company has set aside money for training but we would like to know what the best approach to go about this is?

A: Even before implementing SAP HR, consider the following factors: size of the HR department; current technology used by HR; ROI after the shift in terms of operation, data flow, analysis and integration with other program; current payroll system; other needs assessment factors like functions that also need to be converted to SAP; and lastly time factor for conversions.

Another option to consider is to outsource the HR application. Offshore service is one cost effective alternative.

Question 47: Data Migration

How do you implement data migration in a HR module?

A: SCAT is decommissioned for data migration. However, you can use ECATT. It is available in 4.7 from memory.

Question 48: Download to Excel

How can I download a feature in table format into Excel?

A: The best thing to do is to cut and paste. Use Ctrl-Y>Highlight the area>Ctrl-C>Go to Excel>Ctrl-V.

Question 49: Payroll Run

Our payroll run is currently taking 3 hours to process using the standard schema. How can we shorten a payroll run execution?

A: Check to see if the 'Display Log' parameter has been selected. If it is, this would be the cause in the increased time of payroll run execution. You can also look in PA03 to check if "Earliest Retro Accounting Date" has been set to an appropriate value.

Question 50: Personnel Calculation Rules

Is there an available guide for creating personnel calculation rules? If so, does it group all "Date Based" operations together and contain tips or best practices summary for each construction sequence?

A: There are some websites that could point you in the right direction. For details specifying individual functions and commands:
http://www.insightcp.com/res_19.htm

And

http://www.insightcp.com/res_20.htm

For instructions on the summary page:

http://www.insightcp.com/research.htm

Question 51: Taxable Wage Types

How can one check if a particular wagetype is taxable or not on an Indian payroll?

A: You can use report RPDLGA20. Check the accumulation wagetypes and choose your taxable pay cumulation. This should give you a list of all taxable wagetypes. Another method is to look for the cumulation classes in table T512W.

Question 52: HR Difficulty

What area within HR is the hardest to master? Which one is the most profitable to use?

A: Each user has their own preference but if you gauge from user groups, a toss up will be between payroll and time evaluation.

Question 53: Hiring and Terminating

Is it possible to do hiring and terminating entries on the same day for one individual? I have attempted to do this and I got an error stating:

"Do not enter personnel action for date of hiring/transfer."

Is there a way to go around this?

A: No. These two actions can't be done on the same day for an individual. You have to do the second action on the following day and use IT0041 to record adjusted termination date.

Question 54: Debugging Rules

How can I debug a rule using a step by step output?

A: Place operation 'BREAK' in your rule at the point where you wish to start your analysis.

Question 55: Holiday Calendar

How do I transport a public holiday calendar that I have created?

A: There are two ways to do it. First, check if your calendar dev system and production system are with the same server. If this is the case, then there is no need to transport as the changes to holiday calendar are client independent. Second, it's possible that 'BASIS' could have disabled the 'cross client configuration'. If this is the case, go to SCC4 and enable that.

Question 56: Time Confirmation

We use the HR-mini-master for time confirmations (CATS). In PA30, I used infotypes 0000 and 315 (default values time recording sheet). For some reason the company code in the organizational data is always defaulted and greyed out. How can I change the company code to access the greyed out area?

A: Company codes are usually defaulted based on the assigned Personnel Area. You can check the IMG: Enterprise Structure>Assignment>Human Resources management>Assignment of Personnel Area to Company Code. This can be found in table T500P.

Question 57: Planed Overtime

Is it possible to capture planned overtime in SAP?

A: Unfortunately, there is nothing in SAP called planned overtime. However, you can try and fit this in the DWS (Daily Work Schedule). It is possible that the least of 2007 (approved overtime) and the clock-in and clock-out (2011) infotype will be considered for overtime.

Question 58: Quota Problems

After running PT60 Schema TQTA, I got 3 successful members as a result. I assumed it generated absence quota for those 3 personnel numbers. However, when I checked the PT50 quota overview, there was no amount indicated and all personnel numbers became 0. This is the number I started with by running report RPTQTA00. What went wrong?

A: If the processing is incorrect, review the customizing too. You can also check IT0007. TM00 will only work with TMS-1. You can also try checking the generation rules and verify if you have enabled accrual through Time Evaluation.

Question 59: Infotype IT0024

Is it possible for an infotype IT0024 to allow text and have it copied?

A: No. The two are mutually exclusive.

Question 60: Wage type values

What method can I use if I want to view all the wagetype values for a particular cumulation/processing class?

A: You can check whether PC00_M99DLGA20 meets your requirement.

Question 61: Personnel Rules

How can I use a standard report to copy a previously designed personnel rule to all other clients and to the production server via transport request?

A: You may include PCR in transport request as object PCYS: R3TR PCYS XXXX. Then check se01, se10 for more details.

Question 62: Profile Match

Is it possible to limit the range of objects for which the user is able to run Profile Match up/Requirements Profile in a Manager's Desktop? If I can somehow limit the range of objects, does it affect viewing of other reports as well?

A: There is a lot of information that can guide you through varying levels of user authorization in R/3 online help.

Question 63: Retroactive Accounting

Is it possible to control the behavior when using retroactive accounting? I have created a wagetype using direct evaluation module in infotype 14. The problem is that when retroactive accounting is enabled owing to record changes for other wagetypes, this wagetype gets the impact as well. I did not intend retro for this wage type. How can I control it so that it produces one time amount calculation and updation in RT?

A: Any retro will cause a complete recalculation of the payroll for the retro period with the balance brought forward to the current period. All wagetypes valid in that period will be reprocessed.

If nothing on your "problem" wagetype has been changed, you should get the same result, and no difference should be brought forward.

From the details given, there is a problem with the valuation of your wagetypes in that results are being produced to the original calculation. I suspect that the problem lies when custom module for valuation is used for the purpose.

You can also try the following procedure:

Check view V_T591B where you define wagetypes which also activates retro. 0014 should be activated for retro in T582A.

Question 64: PCL Error

I was running a US payroll for 957 employees when I encountered the following error:

"It is not possible to delete PCL4 for form (F0)". How can this be resolved?

A: This is an authorization issue. You need to write an access rule so that it can log data when you ran a simulation.

Question 65: Time Types

How do we see the results stored in time types?

A: You can run the report RPCLSTB2.

Question 66: Transporting Layouts

How could we make layout that we saved for a query transportable?

A: After saving your layout within the report output, choose Settings>Layout>Layout management. Choose the relevant layout and then Transport.

You could assign your query to a transaction and then default in the relevant layout using a variant.

Question 67: Query

Is it possible to add a Query to the Manager's Desktop?

A: Yes. The first step would be to assign the query to a transaction. Then add the transaction to the Manager's Desktop in the same way that would any other transaction.

To assign a query to a transaction, use transaction SE93. Then create a new parameter transaction. Use transaction START_REPORT and check "skip initial screen". Then within the "screen fields" area, enter the following: D_SREPOVART-REPORTYPE=AQ

Question 68: Custom Infotypes

I have a problem with the custom infotype development. I have recently developed a custom infotype 9000 which has a table control on the single screen (2000). However, when I save after entering the data, the program goes into an infinite PBO-PAI loop. How can this be resolved?

A. One option is to emulate several records via repetitive field group just like in 0008 infotype (main payments). This solution is sufficient only for small number of records. It also depends on the maximal length of infotype record buffer.

There are also special aided ABAP constructs to manipulate repetitive field groups (DO ... VARYING, WHILE ... VARY...).

If you intend to create several infotype records you definitely cannot do it via HR_INFOTYPE_OPERATION the only option is writing directly into internal infotype buffer. There are some subroutines in SAPFP50P subroutine pool: INSERT_INFOTYP, DELETE_INFOTYP, MODIFY_INFOTYP. Note that they all are internal undocumented subroutines and you can use it at your own risk only. Also note that even after a successful database update the system will treat all those records like separate infotype records and would not display them in a single bunch.

Question 69: Infotypes and Users

How do you avoid displaying the infotype to the user?

A: You can set DIALOG_MODE = 'o' for not displaying the infotype (dialogue box).

You can also check the bapireturn of the FM HR_INFOTYPE_OPERATION on its TYPE component rather than on the ID...
IF L_BAPIRETURN-TYPE = 'E'.
Write: / 'errror'.
ELSEIF L_BAPIRETURN-TYPE = 'S'.
Write: / 'success'.
ENDIF.

Question 70: Default Wage Types

How do you process LGMST for default wagetype based on P0008-TRFST or P0001-ANSVH? How do we extend the structure by adding those 2 fields so we can get default WT we need in IT0008 dynpro?

A: You can utilize the user exits ZXPADU01 and ZXPADU02 to handle any cases where the feature doesn't.

This is an SAP supplied User Exit that you can modify for your own purpose.

Example:

ZXPADU01

IF innnn-infty = '0008'

PERFORM process_it0008_pbo USING innnn

CHANGING innnn.

endif.

The routine "... process_IT0008_pbo " can pretty well do/default anything you want.

Question 71: Compensation Management

We need to create additional status in addition to those 5 Standard delivered in compensation management. Is it possible to create additional status and link it to adjustment type?

A: The correct table is T778S. But modifications deeds in that table will affect every SAP HR.

You can also analyze the requirements of your project if it is possible to use some of the existing status or some non used flag in the table PA0380 to create this approval check (you have flags 1, 2, 3 and 4, non used).

Question 72: Employee Overpayment

How can we resolve a situation wherein there is overpayment of an employee in the amount of $5,000+ gross but the net only amounted to $3000? Since it was the company who paid the deductions for taxes, how do we balance this out in installments?

A: Process it all through the payroll.

Work out what the exact gross equivalent of $3000 is and deduct it in the payroll using the original overpaid wage type.

This should balance each other off and records everything properly for your records. You can then continue to deduct at gross for the remaining amount.

The loan infotype might also be worth looking at to achieve the same result, Infotype 45, but you would probably want your wage types to reflect the proper amount at year end.

One thing to watch out is the tax implications by attracting a higher than normal tax deduction due to the higher gross.

Question 73: Approval adjustments

If someone who is in the international headquarters office looks at someone's adjustments for approval and/or activation, will the adjustment appear in the currency of the employee's country or will the manager see their country currency?

A: If you are using MSS, the system will allow the manager to select the currency that they want to see. They also have the choice to see the originating currency. Central reports can be translated back to the reference currency that is set during customizing.

Question 74: MBP Appraisal Transactions

Is it possible to acquire the list of transactions that are used in MBO Appraisals?

A: To set up the appraisal templates you need IMG transaction OOAM.

To create appraisals for employees>APPCREATE, to change> APPCHANGE.

The appraisal document is only shown on IT0025 when it has been completed, not when in progress.

Question 75: Web Appraisal

How can you access the web appraisal form in R/3 (not ESS) without going thru the IMG transaction OOAM ?

A: MBO transaction starts with PHAP_. You may run transaction se93 and search phap_*, then you will get a full list.

These are the most useful ones:

phap_catalog_pa
phap_admin_pa
phap_prepare_pa
phap_create_pa

Part III - Table and Transaction Code References

Appendix A: HR Table Listing

PA* - PA infotype tables
PCL* - HR clusters
PB* - recruitment tables
PCERT - payroll posting runs

Another useful table is CATSDB for CATS, and
PTEX2000 for the CATS transfer table for infotype
2001/2002.

The rest of the HR Tables are as follows:
DD01L Domains
DD02L SAP tables
DD03L Table Fields
DD03T DD: Texts for fields (language dependent)
DD04L Data elements
DD04T R/3 DD: Data element texts
DD05S Foreign key fields
DD06L Pool/cluster structures
DD20L Matchcode Ids
DD24S Fields of a matchcode ID
T000   Clients
T001   Company Codes
T001E Company code-dependent address data
T001P Personnel Areas/Subareas
T012   House banks
T012K House bank accounts
T012T House bank account names
T500L Personnel Country Grouping
T500P Personnel Areas
T500T Personnel Country Groupings

T501   Employee Group
T501T Employee Group Names
T502T Marital Status Designators
T503   Employee Groups / Subgroups
T503K Employee subgroup
T503T Employee Subgroup Names
T504A Benefits - Default Values (NA)
T504B Benefit Option Texts (North America)
T504C Benefit Type (NA)
T504D Benefit Credit Group Amount
T504E Benefit Amount
T504F Benefit Costs
T508A Work Schedule Rules
T508T Texts for Employee Subgroup Groupings for Work Schedules
T510   Pay Scale Groups
T510A Pay Scale Types
T510F Assign Pay Scale > Time Unit, Currency
T510G Pay Scale Areas
T510H Payroll Constants with Regard to Time Unit
T510I Standard Working Hours
T510J Constant Valuations
T510L Levels
T510M Valuation of pay scale groups acc. to hiring date
T510N Pay Scales for Annual Salaries (NA)
T510S Time Wage Type Selection Rule
T510U Pay Scale Groups
T510Y Special Rules for Wage Type Generation
T511   Wage Types
T512R Cumulation Wage Types in Forms
T512S Texts for Cumulation Wage Types in Forms
T512T Wage Type Texts
T512W Wage Type Valuation

T512Z   Permissibility of Wage Types per Infotype
T513   Jobs
T514S Table Name Texts
T514T Field Name Texts
T51D2 Wage Type Classes
T51D3 Reduction Rules
T51D4 Cumulation Rules
T527X Organizational Units
T528B Positions - Work Centers
T528C Wage Type Catalog
T528T Position Texts
T529A Personnel Event
T529F Fast Data Entry for Events
T529T Personnel Event Texts
T52BT Texts For HR Objects
T52C0 Payroll Schemas
T52C1 Payroll Schemas
T52C2 Texts for Personnel Calculation Schemas
T52C3 Texts for Personnel Calculation Schemas
T52C5 Personnel Calculation Rules
T52CC Schema Directory
T52CD Schema Directory
T52CE Directory of Personnel Calculation Rules
T52CT Text Elements
T52CX Cross References via Generated Schemas
T52D1 Valid Processing Classes
T52D2 Valid Values for Processing Classes
T52D3 Valid Evaluation Classes
T52D4 Permitted Values for Evaluation Classes
T52D5 Wage Type Groups
T52D6 Wage Type Group Texts
T52D7 Assign Wage Types to Wage Type Groups
T52D8 Valid Processing Classes - Texts
T52D9 Valid Values for Processing Classes - Texts

T530 Reasons for Events
T530E Reasons for Changes
T530F Reasons for Changes
T530L Wage Types for Special Payments
T530T Event Reason Texts
T531 Deadline Types
T531S Deadline Type Texts
T533 Leave Types
T533T Leave Type Texts
T539A Default Wage Types for Basic Pay
T539J Base Wage Type Valuation
T539R Events for Standard Wage Maintenance
T539S Wage Types for Standard Wage
Maintenance
T548 Date Types
T548S Date Conversion
T548T Date Types
T548Y Date Types
T549A Payroll Areas
T549B Company Features
T549C Decision Trees for Features (Customers)
T549D Feature Directory
T549L Date modifiers
T549M Monthly Assignment: Payroll Period
T549N Period Modifiers
T549O Text for date modifier
T549P Valid Time Units for Payroll Accounting
T549Q Payroll Periods
T549R Period Parameters
T549S Payroll date types
T549T Payroll Areas
T549M Monthly Assignment: Payroll Period
T549N Period Modifiers
T549O Text for date modifier

T549P Valid Time Units for Payroll Accounting
T549Q Payroll Periods
T549R Period Parameters
T549S Payroll date types
T549T Payroll Areas
T554S Absence and Attendance Types
T554T Absence and Attendance Texts
T554V Defaults for Absence Types
T554Y Time Constraints in HR TIME
T555A Time Types
T555B Time Type Designations
T559A Working Weeks
T559B Name of Working Week
T572F Event Texts
T572G Allowed Values for Events
T572H Event Value Texts
T582A Infotypes
T582B Infotypes Which Are Created Automatically
T582S Infotype Texts
T582V Assignment of Infotypes to Views
T582W Assigns Infotype View to Primary Infotype
T582Z Control Table for PA Time Management
T584A Checking Procedures - Infotype Assignment
T588A Transaction Codes
T588B Infotype Menus
T588C Infotype Menus/Info Groups
T588D Infogroups for Events
T588J Screen Header Definition
T588M Infotype Screen Control
T588N Screen Modification for Account Assignment Block
T588O Screen Modification for Assignment Data
T588Q Screen types for fast entry

T588R Selection Reports for Fast Data Entry
T588S Screen Types for Fast Entry
T588T Menu and Infogroup Designations
T588V Business object type
T588W Event types for infotype operations
T588X Cust. composite definition of event types for
IT operations
T588Z Dynamic Events
T591A Subtype Characteristics
T591B Time Constraints for Wage Types
T591S Subtype Texts
T596F HR Subroutines
T596G Cumulation wage types
T596H _Cumulation wage type texts
T596I Calculation rule for cumulation wage types
T596U Conversion Table
T599B Report Classes
T599C Report Classes
T599D Report Categories
T599F Report Classes - Select Options
T777A Building Addresses
T777T Infotypes
T777Z Infotype Time Constraints
T778T Infotypes
T778U Subtypes

Error Messages tables
T100 Messages
T100A Message IDs for T100
T100C Control of messages by the user
T100O Assignment of message to object
T100S Configurable system messages
T100T Table T100A text
T100V Assignment of messages to tables/views

T100W Assign Messages to Workflow
T100X Error Messages: Supplements

Appendix B: Transaction Code Reference

PC00	Run Payroll
PC10	Payroll menu USA
PE00	Starts Transactions PE01,PE02,PE03
PE01	Schemas
PE02	Calculation Rules
PE03	Features
PE04	Create functions and operations
PE51	HR form editor
PRCA	Payroll calendar
PRCT	Current Settings
PRCU	Printing Checks USA
PRD1	Create DME
SM31	Maintain Tables
SM12	Locked Secessions
TSTC	Table lookup
SPRO	IMG
SE16	Data Browser (Table reports)
PP03	PD Tables
PPOM	Change Org Unit
PO13	Maintain Positions
PO03	Maintain Jobs

Appendix C: Structure Reference

Enterprise Structure
- Company code, personnel area and personnel subarea

Personnel Structure
- Employee group, employee subgroup, payroll accounting area

Organization Structure
- Organizational units, jobs and positions

Employees
- Which position does the employee hold?
- What tasks does the employee have?
- Where does the employee work?
- Which public holidays apply to the employee?
- How will the employee be paid?
- What are the employee working hours?
- How much holiday does the emplyee get?

Most important is the allocation of employees to the structures in their enterprise as it is the first step in entering the personal data.
You assign employees in infotype 0001, Organizational Assignment which will include the employees in the
1. enterprise, personnel and organational structures,
2. company code, a personnel area and a payroll area,

3. positions, organizational unit, a job and a cost center.

The personnel area is used exclusively in Personnel Administration and is unique within a client. Each personnel area must be assigned to a company code. The final element of the company structure, also unique to Personnel Administration is the personnel subarea. Grouping are defined for personnel subareas to specify which entries from subsequent settings can be used for employees assigned to a particular company code or personnel area. These groupings directly or indirectly affect Time Management and Payroll Accounting.

Enterprise Structure
123

Groups   **Client**
            Sub-1   Sub-2   Sub-
3   **Company Code**
    Location-1 Location-2   Location-
3 Location-4   **Peronnel Area**
            Headquater   Production   Personnel
Subarea

The administrative personnel structure consists of the following elements:

1. Employee group
2. Employee subgroup
3. Payroll accounting area
4. Organizational key

The organizational personnel structure consists of the following elements:

1. Position
2. Job
3. Organizational unit

In Personnal Administration, you use the object manager to find employees whose data you want to display or edit. The object manager is connected to the following transactions:
- Display HR Master Data (PA20)
- Maintain HR Master Data (PA30)
- Personnel Actions (PA40)

Organizational Key
The organizational key improves the enterprise structure and the personnel structure. You can use an organizational key to carry out a further organizational assignment for employees. The elements company code, personnel area and personnel subarea from the company structure, help to make up the organizational key. The organizational key is a part of the authorization check.

More Transaction Codes

P1B1	Transfer hiring data for applicant
P1B2	Transfer hiring data for applicant
P1B3	Transfer hiring data for applicant
P1B4	Transfer table T588Z, infotype 4000
P1B5	Transfer opt. archive for applicant
P1B6	Transfer hiring data for applicant
P1B7	Conversion T750B
P1OA	Transfer Settings for Opt.Archiving
P201	Transfer T514D/V from Client 000
P2W1	Transfer Incentive Wage Accounting
P2W2	Copy Incentive Wage Forms
P4SW	Release notes BWP
P5P1	Addition of IT0122 to T588B
P5P2	Delete entries in T588B
PA00	Initial PA Master Data Menu
PA03	Maintain Personnel Control Record
PA04	Maintain HR Number Ranges
PA05	Number Range Maintenance: RP_COIFT
PA06	Number Range Maintenance: PD_SEQ_NR
PA07	Maintain Number Range: RP_GARNEM
PA08	Maintain Number Range: RP_GARNSUB
PA09	
PA10	Personnel File
PA20	Display HR Master Data

PA30	Maintain HR Master Data
PA40	Personnel Actions
PA41	Correct Actions
PA42	Fast Entry for Actions
PA46	Import from Resumix
PA47	Export to Resumix
PA48	Hiring from non-SAP system
PA51	Display Time Data
PA53	Display Time Data
PA61	Maintain Time Data
PA62	List Entry of Additional Data
PA63	Maintain Time Data
PA64	Calendar Entry
PA70	Fast Entry
PA71	Fast Entry of Time Data
PA88	Benefits
PA97	Matrix Maintenance
PA98	Compensation Administration
PA99	Compensation Admin. - Release Report
PAAH	Call Ad-Hoc Query
PACA	HR-CH: PF administration
PACB	HR-CH: PF account maintenance
PACC	HR-CH: PF calculator
PACE	HR-CH: Pension fund : Postings
PACK	HR-CH: Pension fund
PACN	Number range maint: HRCHPKONTO
PACP	HR-CH: Pension fund, interface
PACT	PC parameter maintenance
PAJP	Call reporting tree - Japan

PAL1	Create Sales Representative
PAL2	Display Sales Representative
PAL3	Maintain Sales Representative
PAL4	Create Buyer
PAL5	Maintain Buyer
PAL6	Display Buyer
PAR1	Flexible employee data
PAR2	Employee list
PAT1	Personnel Administration infosystem
PAW1	Who is who
PB00	Recruitment
PB04	Number Range Maintenance: RP_PAPL
PB10	Init.entry of applicant master data
PB20	Display applicant master data
PB30	Maintain applicant master data
PB40	Applicant actions
PB50	Display Applicant Activities
PB60	Maintain Applicant Activities
PB80	Evaluate vacancies
PBA0	Evaluate advertisements
PBA1	Applicant index
PBA2	List of applications
PBA3	Applicant vacancy assignment list
PBA4	Receipt of application
PBA5	Recurring tasks: Print letters
PBA6	Recurring tasks: Print letters
PBA7	Recurring tasks: Data transfer
PBA8	Recurring tasks: Transfer data
PBA9	List of planned actions

PBAA	Evaluate recruitment instrument
PBAB	Maintain vacancy assignments
PBAC	Applicant statistics
PBAD	Recurring tasks: Print letters
PBAE	Applicant pool
PBAF	Vacancy assignment list
PBAG	Screening
PBAH	Decision
PBAI	All applicants via qualifications
PBAJ	Recruitment info system
PBAK	Recurring Tasks: Print Labels
PBAL	Bulk processing
PBAM	Variable Applicant List
PBAN	Ad Hoc Query
PBAO	ABAP Query
PBAP	Internal Applicants Via Quals
PBAQ	External Applicants Via Quals
PBAT	Choose SAPscript or WinWord
PBAU	Maintain T750C
PBAV	Display T750C
PBAW	Maintain T750B
PBAX	Display T750B
PBAY	Maintain T750X
PBAZ	Display T750X
PBCX	Cust. Account Assign. Reference (MM)
PBCY	Cust. Account Assign. Reference (FX)
PBCZ	Cust. Account Assign. Reference (DE)
PBW1	Career Center
PBW2	Career Center: Status tracking
PBWW	Customizing standard text in

	WinWord
PC00	Menu for HR Payroll
PC01	Payroll Menu: Germany
PC02	Payroll Menu: Switzerland
PC03	Payroll Menu: Austria
PC04	Payroll Menu: Spain
PC05	Payroll Menu: Netherlands
PC06	Payroll Menu: France
PC07	Payroll menu Canada
PC08	Payroll Menu: Great Britain
PC09	Payroll Menu: Denmark
PC10	Payroll Menu: USA
PC12	Payroll Menu: Belgium
PC14	Payroll Menu: USA
PC16	Payroll Menu: South Africa
PC1A	HR Menu: Payroll for Austria
PC1B	Payroll Menu: Belgium
PC1C	Menu for HR Payroll Switzerland
PC1D	HR Menu: Payroll for Germany
PC1E	HR Menu: Payroll for Spain
PC1F	HR Menu: Payroll for France
PC1G	HR Menu: Payroll for Great Britain
PC1J	HR menu : Payroll for Japan
PC1K	HR Payroll Menu for Canada
PC1L	
PC1M	HR payroll menu Denmark
PC1N	HR NL: Payroll Menu
PC1Q	HR Payroll Menu - Australia
PC1R	HR-SG: Payroll Menu per periods
PC1S	Menu for HR Payroll Sweden

PC1T	HR Payroll Menu for Czech Republic
PC1U	HR Payroll Menu for USA
PC1W	Payroll Menu: South Africa
PC1X	Payroll Menu: International Version
PC22	Payroll Menu: Japan
PC23	Payroll Menu: Sweden
PC25	Payroll Menu: Singapore
PC2A	New Payroll Menu
PC2B	Payroll Menu Yearly
PC2C	Menu for HR Payroll Annual Switz.
PC2D	New Payroll Menu
PC2E	New Payroll Menu
PC2F	Annual Payroll Menu (F)
PC2G	HR Menu: Payroll for Great Britain
PC2J	HR menu : Payroll for Japan
PC2K	New Payroll Menu (Canada)
PC2L	
PC2M	HR-DK: Annual payroll activities
PC2N	HR NL: New Payroll Menu
PC2R	HR-SG: Payroll Menu: Annual
PC2S	Menu for HR Payroll Annual Sweden
PC2T	HR Payroll Menu for Czech Republic
PC2U	New Payroll Menu
PC2W	New Payroll Menu
PC32	Payroll Menu: Mexico
PC34	Payroll Menu for Indonesia
PC3A	Payroll Menu: Other Periods
PC3B	Other periods
PC3C	Menu for RP Payroll Other per Switz.
PC3D	Payroll Menu: Other Periods

PC3E	Payroll Menu: Other Periods
PC3F	Payroll Menu (F): Other periods
PC3G	HR Menu: Payroll for Great Britain
PC3J	HR menu : Payroll for Japan
PC3K	Payroll Menu: Other Periods (CA)
PC3L	
PC3M	Payroll Menu: Other Periods
PC3N	Payroll Menu: Other Periods (NL)
PC3Q	Pay Scale Reclassification Australia
PC3R	Payroll Menu: Other Periods
PC3S	Menu for RP Payroll Other per Sweden
PC3T	HR Payroll Menu for Czech Republic
PC3U	Payroll Menu: Other Periods
PC3W	Payroll Menu: Other Periods
PC4A	New Payroll Menu
PC4B	Independent Period
PC4C	Menu for RP Payroll Other Switz.
PC4D	New Payroll Menu
PC4E	New Payroll Menu
PC4F	Payroll Menu (F): Period-unrelated
PC4G	HR Menu: Payroll for Great Britain
PC4J	HR menu : Payroll for Japan
PC4K	New Payroll Menu (Canada)
PC4L	
PC4N	HR NL: New Payroll Menu
PC4Q	Pay Scale Increase Australia
PC4R	Payroll menue: Period-Independent
PC4S	Menu for RP Payroll Other Sweden
PC4T	HR Payroll Menu for Czech Republic

PC4U	New Payroll Menu
PC4W	New Payroll Menu
PC5J	HR payroll menu (Japan) - SYOYO
PC5Q	Pay Scale Inc. Extended Australia
PC6J	HR payroll menu (Japan) year-end adj
PC7J	HR payroll menu (Japan) - retirement
PC8J	HR payroll menu Social Insurance JP
PC99	International Payroll Menu
PCC0	Maintnce fam.rltd.bonuses Switz.
PCP0	Post accounting data
PDA1	List of part-time work for pensioner
PDA2	Construct transaction data list
PDB1	Release Info 2.1A - Statements
PDB2	Releaseinfo 2.2A Statements
PDF0	Convert form for remun.statement
PDF2	Form table CY 94/95
PDF7	Delete form in customer client
PDF8	Copy form from SAP client
PDF9	Copy forms within customer client
PDI1	Copy Wage Types from Standard Client
PDJ1	HR Change of Year 93/94 (D)
PDJ2	HR Fiscal year change 94/95 D Suppl.
PDJ3	Bill of materials 3.0C
PDJ6	Evaluation/statistic object list
PDJ7	AV96/97 Continued Pay
PDJ8	Part-time work by pensioners
PDK1	Copy W.Types from Standard Clients
PDLK	HR D(G4) Form Tables f. PayrollAcct
PDP0	Table entries for loans

PDS1	Health insurance funds
PDSD	Object list DynMaßn tax D
PDVA	Copy VAG Wage Types for IT 0093
PE00	Starts Transactions PE01,PE02,PE03
PE01	HR: Maintain Payroll Schemas
PE02	HR: Maintain Calculation Rules
PE03	HR: Features
PE04	Creating Functions and Operations
PE51	HR form editor
PEPM	Profile Matchup
PEPP	Profiles
PF01	Test transact.
PF02	Cust. test of value-based IM
PF05	Number Range Maintenance: HRSOBJECT
PFAC	Maintain standard role
PFAL	HR ALE: Distr. infotypes completely
PFCG	Activity Group Maintenance
PFCP	Copy Workflow Tasks
PFCT	Task Catalog
PFCU	Task Customizing
PFOM	Maintain Assignment to SAP Org.Objs
PFOS	Display Assignment to SAP Org.Objs
PFSE	Start PFS from R/3 System
PFSO	User's Organizational Environment
PFT	Maintain Customer Task
PFTC	General Task Maintenance
PFTR	Standard Task for Transaction
PFTS	Standard Task
PFUD	User Master Data Reconciliation

PFWF	Maintain Workflow Task (customer)
PFWS	Maintain workflow template
PGOM	Graphical Structure Maintenance
PI30	PP-PI Options for Release 3.0
PI50	Transfer selected R/2 orders
PI51	Transfer current R/2 orders
PI60	Transfer confirmations to R/2
PID1	HR-ID: Payroll Menu per periods
PID2	HR-ID: Payroll Menu: Annual
PID3	Payroll Menu: Other Periods
PID4	Payroll menue: Period-Independent
PIMN	Human resources information system
PK00	Kanban
PK01	Create control cycle
PK02	Change control cycle
PK03	Display control cycle
PK99	Function Access via Transaction
PKBC	Chnge Container Status with Bar Code
PKC1	Process cost controlling
PKG1	Copy entries for garnishment CA
PKW1	Kanban board WWW
PM00	Menu for HR Reports
PM01	Enhance Infotypes
PM03	Maintain Number Range Features
PM10	Statements Selection
PM11	Statements - Single Data Entry
PM12	Statements - Fast Data Entry
PM13	Statements - Print
PMAR	Change plan for appropriation req.
PMX1	

PMX2	
PMX3	
PMX4	
PO01	Maintain Work Center
PO02	Maintain Training Program
PO03	Maintain Job
PO04	Maintain Business Event Type
PO05	Maintain Business Event
PO06	Maintain Location
PO07	Maintain Resource
PO08	Maintain External Person
PO09	Maintain Business Event Group
PO10	Maintain Organizational Unit
PO11	Maintain Qualification
PO12	Maintain Resource Type
PO13	Maintain Position
PO14	Maintain Task
PO15	Maintain Company
PO16	Maintain Services
PO17	Maintain Requirements Profile
PO18	Maintain Resource Room
PO19	Maintain External Instructor
POI1	Start Download of Master Data
POIL	View Received Data Log
POIM	Start Download of Master Data
POIT	Start Download of Transaction Data
POIU	Start Receiving Changes to Data
POTB	Parameters for OTB
PP01	Maintain Plan Data (menu-guided)
PP02	Maintain Plan Data (Open)

PP03	Maintain Plan Data (Action-Guided)
PP05	Number Ranges
PP06	Number Range Maintenance: HRADATA
PP07	Tasks/Descriptions
PP20	Career and Succession Planning
PP23	PD Cost Planning: Reset Password
PP26	Plan Scenario Administration
PP27	Release of plan scenarios for CO
PP28	PersCostPl: New Scenario
PP29	PersCostPl: Resumption
PP2B	PD CostPl.: Plan Basic Pay Direct
PP2D	PD CostPl1: Delete Payroll Results
PP2P	PD CPl: Plan Payroll Results Direct
PP30	SAP Room Reservations Planning
PP31	SAP Room Reservations Planning: Data
PP32	SAP Room Reservations: Services
PP40	Correspondence
PP61	Shift Planning
PP62	Shift Planning: Requirements Menu
PP63	Requirements Processing
PP64	Choose Plan Version
PP65	Edit an Entry Object
PP66	Shift Planning: Entry Profile
PP68	Shift Planning: Current Settings
PP69	Choose Text for Organizational Unit
PP6A	Personal Shift Plan
PP6B	Attendance List
PP70	Organizational Management
PP72	Shift Planning

PP74	Personnel Cost Planning
PP75	Assessment
PP7S	Organizational Management
PP90	Set Up Organization
PPCI	Copy Infotype
PPCO	Initial Screen: Organizational Plan
PPCP	Career Planning
PPCT	Task Catalog
PPEM	PD: Display Organizational Structure
PPIo	Transfer of Table Entries
PPIS	Human Resources Information System
PPLB	Evaluate Careers
PPME	Change Matrix Organization
PPMM	Personnel Planning
PPMS	Display Matrix Organization
PPO1	Change Cost Center Assignment
PPO2	Display Cost Center Assignment
PPO3	Change Reporting Structure
PPO4	Display Reporting Structure
PPO5	Change Object Indicators (O/S)
PPO6	Change Object Indicators O/S
PPOA	Display Menu Interface (with dyn.)
PPOC	Create Organizational Unit
PPOM	Maintain Organizational Plan
PPOS	Display Organizational Plan
PPPD	Display Profile
PPPE	Area Menu: Personnel Development
PPPM	Change Profile
PPQ1	Find Objects for Qualifications

PPQ2	Find Objects for Requirements
PPQD	Display Qualifications Catalog
PPRL	Change Material When Profile Deleted
PPRP	Reporting: Personnel Development
PPRV	Change Material When Profile Changed
PPSC	Create Structure
PPSM	Change Structure
PPSP	Succession Planning
PPSS	Display Structure
PPST	Structure Evaluation
PPUP	Settings: User Parameters
PQ01	Actions for Work Center
PQ02	Actions for Training Program
PQ03	Actions for Job
PQ04	Actions for Business Event Type
PQ06	Location Actions
PQ07	Resource Actions
PQ08	Actions for External Person
PQ09	Actions for Business Event Group
PQ10	Actions for Organizational Unit
PQ12	Actions for Resource Type
PQ13	Actions for Position
PQ14	Actions for Task
PQ15	Actions for Company
PQ17	Actions for Requirement Profiles
PQ18	Actions for Resource Room
PQ19	Actions for External Instructor
PQAH	Transaction for Ad Hoc Query
PQLV	Australian Leave Processing

PQRD	Redundancies Australia
PQTM	Terminations Australia
PR00	Trip Costs
PR01	Maintain International Travel Data
PR02	Fast Entry : Inter.Trip Costs Data
PR03	Edit Advances
PR04	Edit Weekly Reports
PR05	Receipt Entry
PR10	Number Range Maint.: RP_REINR
PR11	
PR12	Number Range Maint. for Posting Runs
PR71	Customizing Coding Block 1701
PR72	Customizing Coding Block 1702
PR73	Customizing Coding Block 1703
PR90	Initial Screen: Public Sector
PR91	Display: Trips with Periods
PR92	Display: Trips with Periods
PR93	Change: Trips with Periods
PRAA	Automatic Vendor Maintenance
PRAP	Approval of Trips
PRC2	Customizing Coding Block 1200
PRC7	Customizing Coding Block 1700
PRCC	Credit Card Clearing
PRCD	Delete/Copy Trip Countries
PRCT	Current Settings
PRCU	Check Printing USA
PRD1	Create DME
PRDE	Delete/Restore Trip Prov.Variant
PRDH	Employees with Exceeded Trip Days

PRDX	Call Country Version DME Pre.Program
PREC	Trip Costs Accounting Program
PRF0	Standard Form
PRF1	Summarized Form 1
PRF2	Summarized Form 2
PRFI	Posting to Financial Accounting
PRFW	Income-rel.Expenses Statement
PRHD	Maximum Value Delimitation for Meals
PRHH	Scale Maximum Amounts for Meals
PRHP	Scale Per Diems for Meals
PRIN	Index for Personnel Number in Vendor
PRMC	Trip Costs: Feature TRVCT
PRMD	Maintain HR Master Data
PRMF	Trip Costs: Feature TRVFD
PRML	Set Country Grouping via Dialog Box
PRMM	Personnel Actions
PRMS	Display HR Master Data
PRMT	Update Matchcode T
PROF	Profit Center Accounting
PRPD	Delimitation of Per Diems for Meals
PRPY	Transfer to Payroll Accounting
PRRW	Post Accounting Data
PRST	Period Statistics
PRVT	VAT Recovery
PS00	Basic data
PS01	Project Information System
PS02	Operative Structures
PS03	Project Planning

PS04	Project Approval
PS05	Project Execution
PS06	Project Cost Controlling
PS81	Call Up Report Tree PS81 (Ind.Overv)
PS90	Call Up Report Tree PS90 (Overview)
PS91	Call Up Report Tree PS91 (Costs)
PS92	Call Up Report Tree PS92 (Revenues)
PS93	Call Up Report Tree PS93 (Finances)
PS94	Call Up Report Tree PS94 (Line Itms)
PS95	Call Up Report Tree PS95 (Sum.over.)
PS96	Call Up Report Tree PS96 (Sum.costs)
PS97	Call Up Report Tree PS97 (Sum.rev.s)
PS98	Call Up Report Tree PS98 (Sum.fin.)
PSC	PS Basic data: current settings
PSC0	Set Plan Version Valid for Cost Plan
PSC2	PS Op.structures: current settings
PSC3	PS planning: Current settings
PSC5	PS Implementation: Update Settings
PSCP	Set plan version
PSIC	Curr.settings HR information system
PSJ1	Hokensya Santei Adjustment
PSO0	Set Plan Version for OrgManagement
PSO1	Set Aspect for OrgManagement
PSO2	PS System/Database Tools
PSO3	Infotype overview
PSO4	Individual Infotype Maintenance
PSO5	PD: Administration Tools
PSOA	Work Center Reporting
PSOC	Job Reporting
PSOG	OrgManagement General Reporting

PSOI	Tools Integration PA-PD
PSOO	Organizational Unit Reporting
PSOS	Position Reporting
PSOT	Task Reporting
PSSD	Check BNL flow types
PSV0	Change / Display Resources
PSV1	Dynamic Attendance Menu
PSV2	Dynamic Business Event Menu
PSV3	Dynamic Information Menu
PSV4	Set Plan Version
PSV5	Info: Attendances
PSV6	Reporting: Business Events
PSV7	Reporting: Resources
PSV8	Create Attendee
PSV9	Change / Display Attendee
PSVA	Set Aspect
PSVC	Training and Events:Current Settings
PSVL	Set Business Event Language
PSVO	Change / Display Organizer
PSVP	Dynamic Planning Menu
PSVR	Dynamic Resource Menu
PSVT	Dynamic Tool Menu
PT00	Time Management
PT01	Create Work Schedule
PT02	Change Work Schedule
PT03	Display Work Schedule
PT10	
PT11	Number Range Maintenance: PTM_QUONR
PT12	Number Range Maintenance:

	HRAA_PDOC
PT40	PDC Error Transaction
PT41	Communication Parameters
PT42	Supply Personnel Data
PT43	Supply Master Data
PT44	Upload Request
PT45	Post Person Time Events
PT46	Post Working Time Events
PT50	Leave Accrual
PT60	Time Evaluation
PT61	Time Statement
PT62	Attendance List
PT63	Personal Work Schedule
PT64	Absence List
PT65	Graphical Abs./Attendance Overview
PT66	Display Cluster B2
PT67	Third-Party Payroll Accounting
PT68	Activity Allocation
PT70	Time Management Info System
PT71	Tool Selection for Time Management
PT82	CC1: Download HR Mini Master Records
PT83	CC1: Download Employee Time Balances
PT84	Allowed Absence/Attendance Reasons
PT85	Allowed External Wage Types
PT86	Allowed Time Event Types
PT87	Allowed Positions
PTE1	Generate Batch Input Session
PTE2	Process Batch Input Session
PTE3	Reorganize Interface File

PU00	Delete Personnel Data
PU01	Delete current payroll result
PU03	Change Payroll Status
PU11	Supplementary CS Benefits (D)
PU12	Connection to Third-Party Payroll
PU13	Correction Checks
PU14	On Demand Check for Regular Pay
PU15	On Demand Checks (Bonus)
PU20	Preperation for issuing of tax forms
PU21	Issuing of tax forms
PU22	HR Archiving
PU23	SARA parameters set for PA_CALC
PU24	SARA parameters set for PA_TIME
PU25	SARA parameters set for PA-TRAVEL
PU30	Wage Type Maintenance
PU90	Delete applicant data
PU95	HR: Maintain Log. Views & WT Groups
PU96	HR: Maintain Wage Type Groups
PU97	HR: Logical View Maintenance
PU98	Assign Wage Types to Groups
PUC0	HR-CH: Maintain MA attributes
PUCA	HR-CH: PC admin. for PF
PUCE	HR-CH: PC editor for PF
PUCF	HR-CH: PC maintenance form PF
PUCG	HR-CH: Funds-total copier
PUCK	HR-CH: Entity copier for funds
PUCP	HR-CH: PC parameter maint. for PF
PUCV	HR-CH: Entity copier for PC obj.
PUCW	HR-CH: Maint. of HSC outputs for PF

PUG1	HR-GB: On-demand payroll
PULT	Transport HR Tables for Logistics
PUU1	BSI Test Tool
PUUG	Change remittance due date
PV00	Book Attendance
PV01	Rebook Attendance
PV02	Prebook Attendance
PV03	Replace Attendance
PV04	Cancel Attendance
PV05	Book List: Attendees/Business Events
PV06	Prebook List: Attendees
PV07	Book List: Attendees
PV08	Book List: Business Events
PV09	Plan Business Events
PV0I	Display Business Event Offer
PV10	Create Business Event with Resources
PV11	Create Business Event w/o Resources
PV12	Firmly Book / Cancel Business Event
PV14	Lock / Unlock Business Event
PV15	Follow Up Business Event
PV16	Prebooking List per Attendee
PV17	Billing
PV18	Cost Allocation
PV1A	Change Business Event
PV1B	Display Business Event
PV1C	Cost Transfer
PV1D	Price Proposal
PV1I	Attendee Bookings (R/3 Users)
PV26	Prebook List: Attendees/Event Types
PV2I	Attendee Bookings (Web Users)

PV32	Appraisals
PV33	Business Event Appraisal
PV34	Attendee Appraisal
PV3I	Display Business Event Offer
PV4I	Attendee Bookings (Web Users)
PV5I	Attendee Bookings (R/3 Users)
PV6I	Attendee Bookings (Web Users)
PVB0	Business Event Budget
PVB1	Create Business Event Budget
PVB2	Display Business Event Budget
PVB3	Change Business Event Budget
PVBA	Training & Events: Budget Comparison
PVBB	Create/Change Training Program
PVCT	Master Data Catalog
PVD0	Create/Change Business Event Type
PVF0	Create/Change Location
PVF1	Maintain Location
PVG0	Create/Change Resource
PVG1	Create/Change Room
PVG2	Lock/Unlock Resource
PVG3	Maintain Room
PVH0	Create/Change External Instructor
PVH1	Create/Change Instructor
PVH2	Maintain External Person
PVL0	Create/Change Business Event Group
PVMN	Training & Event Management
PVR0	Create/Change Resource Type
PVR1	Maintain Room Equipment
PVU0	Create/Change Company

PVU1	Maintain Company
PVV0	Create/Change Service
PW00	Incentive Wages
PW01	Maintain Incentive Wages Data
PW02	Display Incentive Wages Data
PW03	Enter Incentive Wages Data
PW41	Generate Batch Input Session
PW42	Process Batch Input Session
PW43	Reorganize Interface File
PW61	Time Leveling
PW62	Employment Percentage
PW63	Reassignment of Pay Scale Group
PW70	Recalculate Indiv. Incentive Wages
PW71	Recalculate Group Incentive Wages
PW80	Incentive Wages: Current Settings
PW91	Incentive Wages: Control Parameters
PW92	Incentive Wages: User Exits
PW93	Incentive Wages: Group Parameters
PW94	Inc. Wages: Logistics Parameters
PW95	Incentive Wages: PDC Parameters
PX01	Planning area, external plan. tool
PX02	Planning tool, physical system
PX03	Planning Tool
PX04	Ext.Planning Tool: StartParam. WinNT
PY00	Maintenance T77PR for Rel.Notes 20.A
PY01	Adopt T77R* from release note 20.A
PY02	Adopt T77KL from release notes
PYG1	HR-GB: Config. end of year filepaths
PYG2	HR-GB: Generate EOY cluster